Notes Partners-Relationship Log Book

Notes
Partners-Relationship
Log Book

By Sirron V. Kyles

Notes Partners Relationship Log Book
A Continuation Of The, Dos & Don'ts Of A Committed Relationship's Book

Copyright ©2016
Author Sirron V. Kyles

Bar Code: 787859468964
ISBN: 978-0-9970006-2-7

Cover By Sirron 12
Illustrations: Ariadna Pérez Hernández
Editor: Maria Fernanda Vega Garibay
Book Layout: Vesna Trpkovska

All Rights Reserved. No part of this book may be reproduced in any form, by either electronic or mechanical means, including information storage or retrieval systems, without permission in writing from the publisher. The exception is in reviews that quote brief passages.

Published & Printed In The USA
Publish 2018 HousTone Publishing
PO Box 8305 Houston, Texas 77288 USA

info@houstonepublishing.com * www.houstonepublishing.com
PH-713-866-4006 * 281-605-9299-Fax 713-866-4006

Table of Content

About The Author 7
Author's Preface. 9
Introduction To Notes Partners-Relationship Log. 11
Start Getting Closer Leave Notes Below 15
Tolerance 17
Honesty. 35
Communication 53
Commitment 71
Temptation. 89
Finances 107
Faith 125
Family. 143
Friends 161
Sex. 179
Politics. 197
Conclusion 217

About The Author

Sirron V. Kyles was born in Texas and is best known as the creator of the Bob Marley Festival Tour. One of his many skill sets, he is a Visual Communication Creative Specialist who focuses on Art Décor Corporate & Individual Branding, Photography and Graphic Design. His education consists of certificates from Rice University, Lee Jr. College, San Jose State and degrees from Houston Community Colleges and the Columbia School of Broadcasting. According to Sirron, they each one helped him greatly in writing this book.

He was honorably discharged from the US Navy, which included three tours in Vietnam as a member of the Special Services. In high school he was a member of the ROTC and served on the Houston City Honor Guard, Color Guard and Drill Team, which he feels was very important in helping him establish discipline early in his life. Sirron also played basketball in the Navy, high school, collage and professionally (mostly in the ABA) and was a member of the swim team.

Sirron, said, "I have been involved in many committed relationships over the years, and always considered that I was popular with women."

"Those experiences provided a great deal of insight into the content of this book and the different points of understanding relationships that I may not have been aware of without the time I spent with the women I shared my life with."

Sirron has published several articles and other books that he either authored or coauthored. The Notes-Partners Relationship Log is a continuation of The Dos & Don't Of A Committed Relationship book.

Author's Preface

> *"The reason for writing this book was to share personal information, experiences and solutions from those who are now working through committed relationships, along with research and conversations with others who also have been in committed relationships. When making the decision to enter into a commitment with another person, it should never be taken lightly or made hastily. It is too serious of an undertaking to be based solely on emotions. Most of us would not marry another person without giving it serious consideration; why would you think of making a similar type of commitment without giving it the same amount of common sense reflection?"*

To me, the most important way to start the conversation about the dos and don'ts of a committed relationship is to say that you don't have to believe everything you read in this book, but you might learn something if you do. Take this advice as just relationship information. Everyone's relationship is different and what matters to one person may not be important to another. Still, there are some general dos and don'ts outlined in chapters of this book that may prove very valuable when considering whether or not to enter a committed relationship.

There's always an exception to the rule. For example, things you shouldn't tell your partner:

"My mother thinks you're getting fat."

Or

"Actually, I think Scarlett Johansson/Chris Hemsworth/Tyra Banks/ Chris Evans/ Diego Boneta/Kate Upton/Denzel Washington/Sofia Vergara is way, way hotter than you."

You should use common sense concerning things that harm the relationship. Both parties should discuss past relationships. It may create doubt in their relationship during the beginning, until they get to know each other, but I feel it is best to start with a clean slate.

Tolerance, honesty, communication, sex, faith, commitment, family, temptation, politics, finances and friends all influence how long and strong a committed relationship will be. I know from personal experience that each of them influenced how my committed relationships transpired. I'm sad to say that 75% of those relationships ended as a result of me deciding to let don'ts influence my decisions and clearly not just the fault of the wonderful ladies that chose to make commitments with me - just saying.

There are general dos and don'ts that you can use as guidance in this book, no matter what stage your relationship is in. I only wish I had read a book like this earlier in life. I am sure I would have made wiser decisions in some of my past relationships, but as a result of writing this book, I will make better decisions in future relationships.

Introduction
To Notes-Partners Relationship Log

Have you ever wondered how you can strengthen your relationship with your partner? The Notes-Partners Relationship Log is a continuation of The Dos & Don't Of A Committed Relationship book. Notes-Partners Relationship Log was written to help in the process of achieving this precise goal.

We all want peace in our lives and a, stronger and happier relationships, long lasting love and intimacy. This book covers 11 different informative and interesting topics, formatted too insure intimate contact between both partners: from communication and sex, to friendship, politics and much more; just research the topic that can help you most at the present moment in your relationship, and start creating the life you know you both deserve.

Communication is the key foundation for any strong relationship, but it can often become a struggle between partners. Sensitive subjects are commonly avoided in order to prevent a fight, which leads to partners shutting down, affecting the relationship. This book is about strengthening and rejuvenating your bond; The Notes-Partners Relationship Log provides a vessel that channels those discussions and creates healthy communication habits.

The Notes help partners to interact with each other in a loving, thoughtful manner by discussing different topics, leaving messages to one another in different sections and even choosing between different moods to share feelings. This process is all about creating intimacy, sharing and communicating without the use of phones and the Internet. The Notes encourage a healthy, loving, consistent communication process and create understanding when writing responses.

Sirron V. Kyles the author, created this platform to encourage readers to share their feelings and thoughts in a simple note form; always keeping in mind that you will have to approach this communication tool with an open mind and willingness to respond, trust and always respect each other, no matter what the other writes.

*The Notes are only available in the book's paperback version.

The Notes-Partners Relationship Log allows for partners to become more loving towards each other and in essence become a unit rather than just drift apart. The ultimate goal: thrive in a Committed Relationship.

Samples of what you will find in Notes-Partners Relationship Logs

Name: Bob
Date: Monday
Time: Lunch
Mood: Horny
Comments: I really miss seeing you in your sexy lingerie. You are still hot and I miss the show.

Name: Mary
Date: 7/1
Time: 3PM
Mood: Happy
Comments: I miss it too, it is just that after I had the baby I did not feel sexy anymore and I simply forgot that I had such things around. I will pull them out soon, so be prepared for the show of a lifetime and expect to see the hot me once again.

Name: Mary
Date: 7/7
Time: 8PM
Mood: Wondering
Comments: hey honey, I wanted to let you know that I am really jealous of your new secretary and I thought you should know. Saying it here also felt like the right thing to do so as to avoid loads of accusations and assumptions.

Name: Bob
Date: 7/7
Time: 10PM
Mood: Smiley face
Comments: What! You should have no worries there, as my eyes are only for you and you alone. Even the guys at work often look at you all the time saying how luckier I am to have you.

Name: Mary
Date: 7/7
Time: Midnight
Mood: Blessed
Comments: I love you so much honey! And thank you for loving me too... guys at work looking at me??? Now that is a shocker... Ha! Ha! Ha!

Name: Mary
Date: 7/10
Time: 11 AM
Mood: Kisses
Comments: Hi honey, thanks very much for taking me dancing last night. I had so much fun with you, it really brought up some old memories we have had. Thanks again, love you

Start Getting Closer Leave Notes Below

Tolerance

Tolerance, in reference to this chapter, is about tolerating (or forgiving) actions or poor judgments of a partner that they may not agree with in order to maintain the committed relationship. For couples that have been married for many years, one thing that keeps them together is tolerance and forgiveness of their partner's errors in judgments. The other reasons they chose to show tolerance may have something to do with their fear of being alone or the loss of security they have with their partner.

How many times have you wanted to say something to your partner for the way they were behaving but did not for fear of them taking it the wrong way so you just tolerate their behavior with out saying anything. You can say what you did not say earlier here in Notes; just make sure you partner know you left a note. Keep in mind that you have to approach this communication tool with an open mind and willingness to communicate and trust each other no matter what the other writes as it's simply about strengthening your partnership.

Name:
Date:
Time:
Mood:
Comments:

Name:
Date:
Time:
Mood:
Comments:

Name:
Date:
Time:
Mood:
Comments:

Name:
Date:
Time:
Mood:
Comments:

Name:
Date:
Time:
Mood:
Comments:

Name:
Date:
Time:
Mood:
Comments:

Name:
Date:
Time:
Mood:
Comments:

Name:
Date:
Time:
Mood:
Comments:

Name:
Date:
Time:
Mood:
Comments:

Name:
Date:
Time:
Mood:
Comments:

Name:
Date:
Time:
Mood:
Comments:

Name:
Date:
Time:
Mood:
Comments:

Name:
Date:
Time:
Mood:
Comments:

Name:
Date:
Time:
Mood:
Comments:

Name:
Date:
Time:
Mood:
Comments:

Name:
Date:
Time:
Mood:
Comments:

Name:
Date:
Time:
Mood:
Comments:

Name:
Date:
Time:
Mood:
Comments:

Name:
Date:
Time:
Mood:
Comments:

Name:
Date:
Time:
Mood:
Comments:

Name:
Date:
Time:
Mood:
Comments:

Name:
Date:
Time:
Mood:
Comments:

Name:
Date:
Time:
Mood:
Comments:

Name:
Date:
Time:
Mood:
Comments:

Name:
Date:
Time:
Mood:
Comments:

Name:
Date:
Time:
Mood:
Comments:

Name:
Date:
Time:
Mood:
Comments:

Name:
Date:
Time:
Mood:
Comments:

Name:
Date:
Time:
Mood:
Comments:

Name:
Date:
Time:
Mood:
Comments:

Name:
Date:
Time:
Mood:
Comments:

Name:
Date:
Time:
Mood:
Comments:

Name:
Date:
Time:
Mood:
Comments:

Name:
Date:
Time:
Mood:
Comments:

Name:
Date:
Time:
Mood:
Comments:

Name:
Date:
Time:
Mood:
Comments:

Name:
Date:
Time:
Mood:
Comments:

Name:
Date:
Time:
Mood:
Comments:

Name:
Date:
Time:
Mood:
Comments:

Name:
Date:
Time:
Mood:
Comments:

Name:

Date:

Time:

Mood:

Comments:

Name:

Date:

Time:

Mood:

Comments:

Name:

Date:

Time:

Mood:

Comments:

Name:

Date:

Time:

Mood:

Comments:

Name:
Date:
Time:
Mood:
Comments:

Name:
Date:
Time:
Mood:
Comments:

Name:
Date:
Time:
Mood:
Comments:

Name:
Date:
Time:
Mood:
Comments:

Name:
Date:
Time:
Mood:
Comments:

Name:
Date:
Time:
Mood:
Comments:

Name:
Date:
Time:
Mood:
Comments:

Name:
Date:
Time:
Mood:
Comments:

Name:
Date:
Time:
Mood:
Comments:

Name:
Date:
Time:
Mood:
Comments:

Name:
Date:
Time:
Mood:
Comments:

Name:
Date:
Time:
Mood:
Comments:

Name:
Date:
Time:
Mood:
Comments:

Name:
Date:
Time:
Mood:
Comments:

Name:
Date:
Time:
Mood:
Comments:

Name:
Date:
Time:
Mood:
Comments:

Tolerance

Name:
Date:
Time:
Mood:
Comments:

Name:
Date:
Time:
Mood:
Comments:

Name:
Date:
Time:
Mood:
Comments:

Name:
Date:
Time:
Mood:
Comments:

Honesty

You have to be able to trust your partner, and you earn that trust by being honest yourself. Ground rules should be established at the beginning of the relationship detailing what each person will share about their past, good and bad. Many relations are doomed from the start because of partners sharing things from their past that may not seem like much to them, but may be seen as negative by their partner.

You should get to know your partner before sharing things like how many people you have dated or slept with or, for that matter, how bad your last relationship ended, your dislike for their parents, etc. Keep in mind that you have to approach this communication tool with an open mind and willingness to communicate and trust each other no matter what the other writes as it's simply about strengthening your partnership.

Name:
Date:
Time:
Mood:
Comments:

Name:
Date:
Time:
Mood:
Comments:

Name:
Date:
Time:
Mood:
Comments:

Name:
Date:
Time:
Mood:
Comments:

Name:
Date:
Time:
Mood:
Comments:

Name:
Date:
Time:
Mood:
Comments:

Name:
Date:
Time:
Mood:
Comments:

Name:
Date:
Time:
Mood:
Comments:

Name:

Date:

Time:

Mood:

Comments:

Name:

Date:

Time:

Mood:

Comments:

Name:

Date:

Time:

Mood:

Comments:

Name:

Date:

Time:

Mood:

Comments:

Name:
Date:
Time:
Mood:
Comments:

Name:
Date:
Time:
Mood:
Comments:

Name:
Date:
Time:
Mood:
Comments:

Name:
Date:
Time:
Mood:
Comments:

Name:
Date:
Time:
Mood:
Comments:

Name:
Date:
Time:
Mood:
Comments:

Name:
Date:
Time:
Mood:
Comments:

Name:
Date:
Time:
Mood:
Comments:

Name:
Date:
Time:
Mood:
Comments:

Name:
Date:
Time:
Mood:
Comments:

Name:
Date:
Time:
Mood:
Comments:

Name:
Date:
Time:
Mood:
Comments:

Name:
Date:
Time:
Mood:
Comments:

Name:
Date:
Time:
Mood:
Comments:

Name:
Date:
Time:
Mood:
Comments:

Name:
Date:
Time:
Mood:
Comments:

Name:
Date:
Time:
Mood:
Comments:

Name:
Date:
Time:
Mood:
Comments:

Name:
Date:
Time:
Mood:
Comments:

Name:
Date:
Time:
Mood:
Comments:

Name:
Date:
Time:
Mood:
Comments:

Name:
Date:
Time:
Mood:
Comments:

Name:
Date:
Time:
Mood:
Comments:

Name:
Date:
Time:
Mood:
Comments:

Name:
Date:
Time:
Mood:
Comments:

Name:
Date:
Time:
Mood:
Comments:

Name:
Date:
Time:
Mood:
Comments:

Name:
Date:
Time:
Mood:
Comments:

Name:
Date:
Time:
Mood:
Comments:

Name:
Date:
Time:
Mood:
Comments:

Name:
Date:
Time:
Mood:
Comments:

Name:
Date:
Time:
Mood:
Comments:

Name:
Date:
Time:
Mood:
Comments:

Name:
Date:
Time:
Mood:
Comments:

Name:
Date:
Time:
Mood:
Comments:

Name:
Date:
Time:
Mood:
Comments:

Name:
Date:
Time:
Mood:
Comments:

Name:
Date:
Time:
Mood:
Comments:

Name:
Date:
Time:
Mood:
Comments:

Name:
Date:
Time:
Mood:
Comments:

Name:
Date:
Time:
Mood:
Comments:

Name:
Date:
Time:
Mood:
Comments:

Name:
Date:
Time:
Mood:
Comments:

Name:
Date:
Time:
Mood:
Comments:

Name:
Date:
Time:
Mood:
Comments:

Name:
Date:
Time:
Mood:
Comments:

Name:
Date:
Time:
Mood:
Comments:

Name:
Date:
Time:
Mood:
Comments:

Name:
Date:
Time:
Mood:
Comments:

Name:
Date:
Time:
Mood:
Comments:

Name:
Date:
Time:
Mood:
Comments:

Name:
Date:
Time:
Mood:
Comments:

Communication

Communication is one of the most important aspects of a committed relationship, but you don't always have to tell your partner everything – as I stated previously. At the same time, you don't get to know each other without communication, no matter how nice other aspects of your relationship are.

You don't build something that will last if you don't know your partner. Communication is critical in creating a truly long-lasting relationship between two partners; without it, the relationship is doomed to fail. Keep in mind that you have to approach this communication tool with an open mind and willingness to communicate and trust each other no matter what the other writes as it's simply about strengthening your partnership.

Name:
Date:
Time:
Mood:
Comments:

Name:
Date:
Time:
Mood:
Comments:

Name:
Date:
Time:
Mood:
Comments:

Name:
Date:
Time:
Mood:
Comments:

Name:
Date:
Time:
Mood:
Comments:

Name:
Date:
Time:
Mood:
Comments:

Name:
Date:
Time:
Mood:
Comments:

Name:
Date:
Time:
Mood:
Comments:

Name:
Date:
Time:
Mood:
Comments:

Name:
Date:
Time:
Mood:
Comments:

Name:
Date:
Time:
Mood:
Comments:

Name:
Date:
Time:
Mood:
Comments:

Communication

Name:
Date:
Time:
Mood:
Comments:

Name:
Date:
Time:
Mood:
Comments:

Name:
Date:
Time:
Mood:
Comments:

Name:
Date:
Time:
Mood:
Comments:

Name:
Date:
Time:
Mood:
Comments:

Name:
Date:
Time:
Mood:
Comments:

Name:
Date:
Time:
Mood:
Comments:

Name:
Date:
Time:
Mood:
Comments:

Name:
Date:
Time:
Mood:
Comments:

Name:
Date:
Time:
Mood:
Comments:

Name:
Date:
Time:
Mood:
Comments:

Name:
Date:
Time:
Mood:
Comments:

Name:
Date:
Time:
Mood:
Comments:

Name:
Date:
Time:
Mood:
Comments:

Name:
Date:
Time:
Mood:
Comments:

Name:
Date:
Time:
Mood:
Comments:

Name:
Date:
Time:
Mood:
Comments:

Name:
Date:
Time:
Mood:
Comments:

Name:
Date:
Time:
Mood:
Comments:

Name:
Date:
Time:
Mood:
Comments:

Name:
Date:
Time:
Mood:
Comments:

Name:
Date:
Time:
Mood:
Comments:

Name:
Date:
Time:
Mood:
Comments:

Name:
Date:
Time:
Mood:
Comments:

Communication

Name:
Date:
Time:
Mood:
Comments:

Name:
Date:
Time:
Mood:
Comments:

Name:
Date:
Time:
Mood:
Comments:

Name:
Date:
Time:
Mood:
Comments:

Name:
Date:
Time:
Mood:
Comments:

Name:
Date:
Time:
Mood:
Comments:

Name:
Date:
Time:
Mood:
Comments:

Name:
Date:
Time:
Mood:
Comments:

Name:
Date:
Time:
Mood:
Comments:

Name:
Date:
Time:
Mood:
Comments:

Name:
Date:
Time:
Mood:
Comments:

Name:
Date:
Time:
Mood:
Comments:

Name:
Date:
Time:
Mood:
Comments:

Name:
Date:
Time:
Mood:
Comments:

Name:
Date:
Time:
Mood:
Comments:

Name:
Date:
Time:
Mood:
Comments:

Name:
Date:
Time:
Mood:
Comments:

Name:
Date:
Time:
Mood:
Comments:

Name:
Date:
Time:
Mood:
Comments:

Name:
Date:
Time:
Mood:
Comments:

Name:
Date:
Time:
Mood:
Comments:

Name:
Date:
Time:
Mood:
Comments:

Name:
Date:
Time:
Mood:
Comments:

Name:
Date:
Time:
Mood:
Comments:

Name:
Date:
Time:
Mood:
Comments:

Name:
Date:
Time:
Mood:
Comments:

Name:
Date:
Time:
Mood:
Comments:

Name:
Date:
Time:
Mood:
Comments:

Commitment

My feeling is that everyone in a serious relationship understands the definition of commitment. I will say that if you decide to enter into a committed relationship, it should be done using not only your emotions, but also logic, while understanding that you want to enjoy your life with another person for an extended period of time. Just Saying.

Keep in mind that you have to approach this communication tool with an open mind and willingness to communicate and trust the feelings of each other no matter what the other writes as it's simply about strengthening your partnership. Notes will enhance your communication in your relationship if you use it.

Name:
Date:
Time:
Mood:
Comments:

Name:
Date:
Time:
Mood:
Comments:

Name:
Date:
Time:
Mood:
Comments:

Name:
Date:
Time:
Mood:
Comments:

Name:
Date:
Time:
Mood:
Comments:

Name:
Date:
Time:
Mood:
Comments:

Name:
Date:
Time:
Mood:
Comments:

Name:
Date:
Time:
Mood:
Comments:

Name:
Date:
Time:
Mood:
Comments:

Name:
Date:
Time:
Mood:
Comments:

Name:
Date:
Time:
Mood:
Comments:

Name:
Date:
Time:
Mood:
Comments:

Name:
Date:
Time:
Mood:
Comments:

Name:
Date:
Time:
Mood:
Comments:

Name:
Date:
Time:
Mood:
Comments:

Name:
Date:
Time:
Mood:
Comments:

Name:
Date:
Time:
Mood:
Comments:

Name:
Date:
Time:
Mood:
Comments:

Name:
Date:
Time:
Mood:
Comments:

Name:
Date:
Time:
Mood:
Comments:

Name:
Date:
Time:
Mood:
Comments:

Name:
Date:
Time:
Mood:
Comments:

Name:
Date:
Time:
Mood:
Comments:

Name:
Date:
Time:
Mood:
Comments:

Name:
Date:
Time:
Mood:
Comments:

Name:
Date:
Time:
Mood:
Comments:

Name:
Date:
Time:
Mood:
Comments:

Name:
Date:
Time:
Mood:
Comments:

Name:
Date:
Time:
Mood:
Comments:

Name:
Date:
Time:
Mood:
Comments:

Name:
Date:
Time:
Mood:
Comments:

Name:
Date:
Time:
Mood:
Comments:

Name:
Date:
Time:
Mood:
Comments:

Name:
Date:
Time:
Mood:
Comments:

Name:
Date:
Time:
Mood:
Comments:

Name:
Date:
Time:
Mood:
Comments:

Commitment

Name:
Date:
Time:
Mood:
Comments:

Name:
Date:
Time:
Mood:
Comments:

Name:
Date:
Time:
Mood:
Comments:

Name:
Date:
Time:
Mood:
Comments:

Name:
Date:
Time:
Mood:
Comments:

Name:
Date:
Time:
Mood:
Comments:

Name:
Date:
Time:
Mood:
Comments:

Name:
Date:
Time:
Mood:
Comments:

Name:
Date:
Time:
Mood:
Comments:

Name:
Date:
Time:
Mood:
Comments:

Name:
Date:
Time:
Mood:
Comments:

Name:
Date:
Time:
Mood:
Comments:

Name:
Date:
Time:
Mood:
Comments:

Name:
Date:
Time:
Mood:
Comments:

Name:
Date:
Time:
Mood:
Comments:

Name:
Date:
Time:
Mood:
Comments:

Name:
Date:
Time:
Mood:
Comments:

Name:
Date:
Time:
Mood:
Comments:

Name:
Date:
Time:
Mood:
Comments:

Name:
Date:
Time:
Mood:
Comments:

Name:
Date:
Time:
Mood:
Comments:

Name:
Date:
Time:
Mood:
Comments:

Name:
Date:
Time:
Mood:
Comments:

Name:
Date:
Time:
Mood:
Comments:

Name:
Date:
Time:
Mood:
Comments:

Name:
Date:
Time:
Mood:
Comments:

Name:
Date:
Time:
Mood:
Comments:

Name:
Date:
Time:
Mood:
Comments:

Temptation

It happens to almost everyone. You meet someone by chance and they're really friendly and funny. You may have had a couple of drinks and you see a great looking person that catches your eye, forgetting for a moment that you're with a committed partner; You; just stare... Notes are away to discuss these types of awkward events.

Keep in mind that you have to approach this communication tool with an open mind and willingness to communicate and trust each other no matter what the other writes, as it's simply about strengthening your partnership.

Name:
Date:
Time:
Mood:
Comments:

Name:
Date:
Time:
Mood:
Comments:

Name:
Date:
Time:
Mood:
Comments:

Name:
Date:
Time:
Mood:
Comments:

Name:
Date:
Time:
Mood:
Comments:

Name:
Date:
Time:
Mood:
Comments:

Name:
Date:
Time:
Mood:
Comments:

Name:
Date:
Time:
Mood:
Comments:

Name:
Date:
Time:
Mood:
Comments:

Name:
Date:
Time:
Mood:
Comments:

Name:
Date:
Time:
Mood:
Comments:

Name:
Date:
Time:
Mood:
Comments:

Temptation

Name:
Date:
Time:
Mood:
Comments:

Name:
Date:
Time:
Mood:
Comments:

Name:
Date:
Time:
Mood:
Comments:

Name:
Date:
Time:
Mood:
Comments:

Name:
Date:
Time:
Mood:
Comments:

Name:
Date:
Time:
Mood:
Comments:

Name:
Date:
Time:
Mood:
Comments:

Name:
Date:
Time:
Mood:
Comments:

Name:
Date:
Time:
Mood:
Comments:

Name:
Date:
Time:
Mood:
Comments:

Name:
Date:
Time:
Mood:
Comments:

Name:
Date:
Time:
Mood:
Comments:

Name:
Date:
Time:
Mood:
Comments:

Name:
Date:
Time:
Mood:
Comments:

Name:
Date:
Time:
Mood:
Comments:

Name:
Date:
Time:
Mood:
Comments:

Name:
Date:
Time:
Mood:
Comments:

Name:
Date:
Time:
Mood:
Comments:

Name:
Date:
Time:
Mood:
Comments:

Name:
Date:
Time:
Mood:
Comments:

Name:

Date:

Time:

Mood:

Comments:

Name:

Date:

Time:

Mood:

Comments:

Name:

Date:

Time:

Mood:

Comments:

Name:

Date:

Time:

Mood:

Comments:

Name:
Date:
Time:
Mood:
Comments:

Name:
Date:
Time:
Mood:
Comments:

Name:
Date:
Time:
Mood:
Comments:

Name:
Date:
Time:
Mood:
Comments:

Name:
Date:
Time:
Mood:
Comments:

Name:
Date:
Time:
Mood:
Comments:

Name:
Date:
Time:
Mood:
Comments:

Name:
Date:
Time:
Mood:
Comments:

Name:
Date:
Time:
Mood:
Comments:

Name:
Date:
Time:
Mood:
Comments:

Name:
Date:
Time:
Mood:
Comments:

Name:
Date:
Time:
Mood:
Comments:

Name:
Date:
Time:
Mood:
Comments:

Name:
Date:
Time:
Mood:
Comments:

Name:
Date:
Time:
Mood:
Comments:

Name:
Date:
Time:
Mood:
Comments:

Name:
Date:
Time:
Mood:
Comments:

Name:
Date:
Time:
Mood:
Comments:

Name:
Date:
Time:
Mood:
Comments:

Name:
Date:
Time:
Mood:
Comments:

Name:
Date:
Time:
Mood:
Comments:

Name:
Date:
Time:
Mood:
Comments:

Name:
Date:
Time:
Mood:
Comments:

Name:
Date:
Time:
Mood:
Comments:

Name:
Date:
Time:
Mood:
Comments:

Name:
Date:
Time:
Mood:
Comments:

Name:
Date:
Time:
Mood:
Comments:

Name:
Date:
Time:
Mood:
Comments:

Finance

In an ideal world, money wouldn't matter with you and your partner. In the real world, unfortunately, we have to deal with lack of funds, disparities between partners, unexpected bills and emergencies. You may commit to a partner that is very wealthy and wants to shower you with material things that could sway your judgment and decisions. Are you could be in a relationship that struggles finically that could turn into blame game.

Either way you and your partner have to manage your finances. This is where sharing your feeling in Notes can offers an easer solution to working through those trying times.

Always keep in mind that you have to approach this communication tool with an open mind and willingness to communicate and trust each other no matter what the other writes as it's simply about strengthening your partnership.

Name:
Date:
Time:
Mood:
Comments:

Name:
Date:
Time:
Mood:
Comments:

Name:
Date:
Time:
Mood:
Comments:

Name:
Date:
Time:
Mood:
Comments:

Name:
Date:
Time:
Mood:
Comments:

Name:
Date:
Time:
Mood:
Comments:

Name:
Date:
Time:
Mood:
Comments:

Name:
Date:
Time:
Mood:
Comments:

Name:

Date:

Time:

Mood:

Comments:

Name:

Date:

Time:

Mood:

Comments:

Name:

Date:

Time:

Mood:

Comments:

Name:

Date:

Time:

Mood:

Comments:

Name:
Date:
Time:
Mood:
Comments:

Name:
Date:
Time:
Mood:
Comments:

Name:
Date:
Time:
Mood:
Comments:

Name:
Date:
Time:
Mood:
Comments:

Name:
Date:
Time:
Mood:
Comments:

Name:
Date:
Time:
Mood:
Comments:

Name:
Date:
Time:
Mood:
Comments:

Name:
Date:
Time:
Mood:
Comments:

Name:
Date:
Time:
Mood:
Comments:

Name:
Date:
Time:
Mood:
Comments:

Name:
Date:
Time:
Mood:
Comments:

Name:
Date:
Time:
Mood:
Comments:

Name:
Date:
Time:
Mood:
Comments:

Name:
Date:
Time:
Mood:
Comments:

Name:
Date:
Time:
Mood:
Comments:

Name:
Date:
Time:
Mood:
Comments:

Name:
Date:
Time:
Mood:
Comments:

Name:
Date:
Time:
Mood:
Comments:

Name:
Date:
Time:
Mood:
Comments:

Name:
Date:
Time:
Mood:
Comments:

Name:

Date:

Time:

Mood:

Comments:

Name:

Date:

Time:

Mood:

Comments:

Name:

Date:

Time:

Mood:

Comments:

Name:

Date:

Time:

Mood:

Comments:

Name:
Date:
Time:
Mood:
Comments:

Name:
Date:
Time:
Mood:
Comments:

Name:
Date:
Time:
Mood:
Comments:

Name:
Date:
Time:
Mood:
Comments:

Name:
Date:
Time:
Mood:
Comments:

Name:
Date:
Time:
Mood:
Comments:

Name:
Date:
Time:
Mood:
Comments:

Name:
Date:
Time:
Mood:
Comments:

Name:
Date:
Time:
Mood:
Comments:

Name:
Date:
Time:
Mood:
Comments:

Name:
Date:
Time:
Mood:
Comments:

Name:
Date:
Time:
Mood:
Comments:

Name:
Date:
Time:
Mood:
Comments:

Name:
Date:
Time:
Mood:
Comments:

Name:
Date:
Time:
Mood:
Comments:

Name:
Date:
Time:
Mood:
Comments:

Name:
Date:
Time:
Mood:
Comments:

Name:
Date:
Time:
Mood:
Comments:

Name:
Date:
Time:
Mood:
Comments:

Name:
Date:
Time:
Mood:
Comments:

Name:

Date:

Time:

Mood:

Comments:

Name:

Date:

Time:

Mood:

Comments:

Name:

Date:

Time:

Mood:

Comments:

Name:

Date:

Time:

Mood:

Comments:

Name:
Date:
Time:
Mood:
Comments:

Name:
Date:
Time:
Mood:
Comments:

Name:
Date:
Time:
Mood:
Comments:

Name:
Date:
Time:
Mood:
Comments:

Faith

You don't have to share your partner's faith, but you do have to acknowledge that widely differing views could be a problem. Older generation's faith was a nonstarter with many long-term relationships.

Often, depending on the faith, couples were not allowed to marry outside of their religion. That meant one of the partners would have to compromise their faith in order to enter into a committed relationship; be thankful, that's not the case today.

Keep in mind that you have to approach this communication tool with an open mind and willingness to communicate and trust each other no matter what the other writes, as it's simply about strengthening your partnership.

Name:

Date:

Time:

Mood:

Comments:

Name:

Date:

Time:

Mood:

Comments:

Name:

Date:

Time:

Mood:

Comments:

Name:

Date:

Time:

Mood:

Comments:

Name:
Date:
Time:
Mood:
Comments:

Name:
Date:
Time:
Mood:
Comments:

Name:
Date:
Time:
Mood:
Comments:

Name:
Date:
Time:
Mood:
Comments:

Name:

Date:

Time:

Mood:

Comments:

Name:

Date:

Time:

Mood:

Comments:

Name:

Date:

Time:

Mood:

Comments:

Name:

Date:

Time:

Mood:

Comments:

Name:
Date:
Time:
Mood:
Comments:

Name:
Date:
Time:
Mood:
Comments:

Name:
Date:
Time:
Mood:
Comments:

Name:
Date:
Time:
Mood:
Comments:

Name:
Date:
Time:
Mood:
Comments:

Name:
Date:
Time:
Mood:
Comments:

Name:
Date:
Time:
Mood:
Comments:

Name:
Date:
Time:
Mood:
Comments:

Name:
Date:
Time:
Mood:
Comments:

Name:
Date:
Time:
Mood:
Comments:

Name:
Date:
Time:
Mood:
Comments:

Name:
Date:
Time:
Mood:
Comments:

Name:
Date:
Time:
Mood:
Comments:

Name:
Date:
Time:
Mood:
Comments:

Name:
Date:
Time:
Mood:
Comments:

Name:
Date:
Time:
Mood:
Comments:

Name:
Date:
Time:
Mood:
Comments:

Name:
Date:
Time:
Mood:
Comments:

Name:
Date:
Time:
Mood:
Comments:

Name:
Date:
Time:
Mood:
Comments:

Name:
Date:
Time:
Mood:
Comments:

Name:
Date:
Time:
Mood:
Comments:

Name:
Date:
Time:
Mood:
Comments:

Name:
Date:
Time:
Mood:
Comments:

Name:
Date:
Time:
Mood:
Comments:

Name:
Date:
Time:
Mood:
Comments:

Name:
Date:
Time:
Mood:
Comments:

Name:
Date:
Time:
Mood:
Comments:

Name:
Date:
Time:
Mood:
Comments:

Name:
Date:
Time:
Mood:
Comments:

Name:
Date:
Time:
Mood:
Comments:

Name:
Date:
Time:
Mood:
Comments:

Name:
Date:
Time:
Mood:
Comments:

Name:
Date:
Time:
Mood:
Comments:

Name:
Date:
Time:
Mood:
Comments:

Name:
Date:
Time:
Mood:
Comments:

Name:
Date:
Time:
Mood:
Comments:

Name:
Date:
Time:
Mood:
Comments:

Name:
Date:
Time:
Mood:
Comments:

Name:
Date:
Time:
Mood:
Comments:

Name:
Date:
Time:
Mood:
Comments:

Name:
Date:
Time:
Mood:
Comments:

Name:
Date:
Time:
Mood:
Comments:

Name:
Date:
Time:
Mood:
Comments:

Name:

Date:

Time:

Mood:

Comments:

Name:

Date:

Time:

Mood:

Comments:

Name:

Date:

Time:

Mood:

Comments:

Name:

Date:

Time:

Mood:

Comments:

Name:
Date:
Time:
Mood:
Comments:

Name:
Date:
Time:
Mood:
Comments:

Name:
Date:
Time:
Mood:
Comments:

Name:
Date:
Time:
Mood:
Comments:

Family

Since we're speaking of family… there are a lot of issues that can come up in this area. Your parents can like or dislike your partner, your sibling might like your partner a bit too much and that's before you even start worrying about what their family thinks of you.

The decision to have children, how many and when also comes into play during long-term, committed relationships. Here's where Notes can be a blessing as it provides a way to remind partners of their special Faith days with each and discuss other related topics by just leaving Notes.

Keep in mind that you have to approach this communication tool with an open mind and willingness to communicate and trust each other no matter what the other writes, as it's simply about strengthening your partnership.

Name:
Date:
Time:
Mood:
Comments:

Name:
Date:
Time:
Mood:
Comments:

Name:
Date:
Time:
Mood:
Comments:

Name:
Date:
Time:
Mood:
Comments:

Name:
Date:
Time:
Mood:
Comments:

Name:
Date:
Time:
Mood:
Comments:

Name:
Date:
Time:
Mood:
Comments:

Name:
Date:
Time:
Mood:
Comments:

Name:

Date:

Time:

Mood:

Comments:

Name:

Date:

Time:

Mood:

Comments:

Name:

Date:

Time:

Mood:

Comments:

Name:

Date:

Time:

Mood:

Comments:

Name:
Date:
Time:
Mood:
Comments:

Name:
Date:
Time:
Mood:
Comments:

Name:
Date:
Time:
Mood:
Comments:

Name:
Date:
Time:
Mood:
Comments:

Name:

Date:

Time:

Mood:

Comments:

Name:

Date:

Time:

Mood:

Comments:

Name:

Date:

Time:

Mood:

Comments:

Name:

Date:

Time:

Mood:

Comments:

Name:
Date:
Time:
Mood:
Comments:

Name:
Date:
Time:
Mood:
Comments:

Name:
Date:
Time:
Mood:
Comments:

Name:
Date:
Time:
Mood:
Comments:

Name:
Date:
Time:
Mood:
Comments:

Name:
Date:
Time:
Mood:
Comments:

Name:
Date:
Time:
Mood:
Comments:

Name:
Date:
Time:
Mood:
Comments:

Name:
Date:
Time:
Mood:
Comments:

Name:
Date:
Time:
Mood:
Comments:

Name:
Date:
Time:
Mood:
Comments:

Name:
Date:
Time:
Mood:
Comments:

Name:
Date:
Time:
Mood:
Comments:

Name:
Date:
Time:
Mood:
Comments:

Name:
Date:
Time:
Mood:
Comments:

Name:
Date:
Time:
Mood:
Comments:

Name:
Date:
Time:
Mood:
Comments:

Name:
Date:
Time:
Mood:
Comments:

Name:
Date:
Time:
Mood:
Comments:

Name:
Date:
Time:
Mood:
Comments:

Name:

Date:

Time:

Mood:

Comments:

Name:

Date:

Time:

Mood:

Comments:

Name:

Date:

Time:

Mood:

Comments:

Name:

Date:

Time:

Mood:

Comments:

Name:
Date:
Time:
Mood:
Comments:

Name:
Date:
Time:
Mood:
Comments:

Name:
Date:
Time:
Mood:
Comments:

Name:
Date:
Time:
Mood:
Comments:

Name:
Date:
Time:
Mood:
Comments:

Name:
Date:
Time:
Mood:
Comments:

Name:
Date:
Time:
Mood:
Comments:

Name:
Date:
Time:
Mood:
Comments:

Name:
Date:
Time:
Mood:
Comments:

Name:
Date:
Time:
Mood:
Comments:

Name:
Date:
Time:
Mood:
Comments:

Name:
Date:
Time:
Mood:
Comments:

Name:
Date:
Time:
Mood:
Comments:

Name:
Date:
Time:
Mood:
Comments:

Name:
Date:
Time:
Mood:
Comments:

Name:
Date:
Time:
Mood:
Comments:

Name:
Date:
Time:
Mood:
Comments:

Name:
Date:
Time:
Mood:
Comments:

Name:
Date:
Time:
Mood:
Comments:

Name:
Date:
Time:
Mood:
Comments:

Friends

The foundation of any committed relationship is based on friendship; many relationships begin with the heat of sexual emotions, but after spending and extensive amount of time with that person you find out that you are not compatible as friends. You may have discovered sooner had you use Notes as part of getting to know each other; Just Saying Keep in mind that you have to approach this communication tool with an open mind and willingness to communicate and trust each other no matter what the other writes as it's simply about strengthening your partnership.

Name:
Date:
Time:
Mood:
Comments:

Name:
Date:
Time:
Mood:
Comments:

Name:
Date:
Time:
Mood:
Comments:

Name:
Date:
Time:
Mood:
Comments:

Name:
Date:
Time:
Mood:
Comments:

Name:
Date:
Time:
Mood:
Comments:

Name:
Date:
Time:
Mood:
Comments:

Name:
Date:
Time:
Mood:
Comments:

Name:
Date:
Time:
Mood:
Comments:

Name:
Date:
Time:
Mood:
Comments:

Name:
Date:
Time:
Mood:
Comments:

Name:
Date:
Time:
Mood:
Comments:

Name:
Date:
Time:
Mood:
Comments:

Name:
Date:
Time:
Mood:
Comments:

Name:
Date:
Time:
Mood:
Comments:

Name:
Date:
Time:
Mood:
Comments:

Name:

Date:

Time:

Mood:

Comments:

Name:

Date:

Time:

Mood:

Comments:

Name:

Date:

Time:

Mood:

Comments:

Name:

Date:

Time:

Mood:

Comments:

Name:
Date:
Time:
Mood:
Comments:

Name:
Date:
Time:
Mood:
Comments:

Name:
Date:
Time:
Mood:
Comments:

Name:
Date:
Time:
Mood:
Comments:

Name:
Date:
Time:
Mood:
Comments:

Name:
Date:
Time:
Mood:
Comments:

Name:
Date:
Time:
Mood:
Comments:

Name:
Date:
Time:
Mood:
Comments:

Name:
Date:
Time:
Mood:
Comments:

Name:
Date:
Time:
Mood:
Comments:

Name:
Date:
Time:
Mood:
Comments:

Name:
Date:
Time:
Mood:
Comments:

Name:
Date:
Time:
Mood:
Comments:

Name:
Date:
Time:
Mood:
Comments:

Name:
Date:
Time:
Mood:
Comments:

Name:
Date:
Time:
Mood:
Comments:

Name:
Date:
Time:
Mood:
Comments:

Name:
Date:
Time:
Mood:
Comments:

Name:
Date:
Time:
Mood:
Comments:

Name:
Date:
Time:
Mood:
Comments:

Name:

Date:

Time:

Mood:

Comments:

Name:

Date:

Time:

Mood:

Comments:

Name:

Date:

Time:

Mood:

Comments:

Name:

Date:

Time:

Mood:

Comments:

Name:
Date:
Time:
Mood:
Comments:

Name:
Date:
Time:
Mood:
Comments:

Name:
Date:
Time:
Mood:
Comments:

Name:
Date:
Time:
Mood:
Comments:

Name:
Date:
Time:
Mood:
Comments:

Name:
Date:
Time:
Mood:
Comments:

Name:
Date:
Time:
Mood:
Comments:

Name:
Date:
Time:
Mood:
Comments:

Name:
Date:
Time:
Mood:
Comments:

Name:
Date:
Time:
Mood:
Comments:

Name:
Date:
Time:
Mood:
Comments:

Name:
Date:
Time:
Mood:
Comments:

Name:

Date:

Time:

Mood:

Comments:

Name:

Date:

Time:

Mood:

Comments:

Name:

Date:

Time:

Mood:

Comments:

Name:

Date:

Time:

Mood:

Comments:

Name:
Date:
Time:
Mood:
Comments:

Name:
Date:
Time:
Mood:
Comments:

Name:
Date:
Time:
Mood:
Comments:

Name:
Date:
Time:
Mood:
Comments:

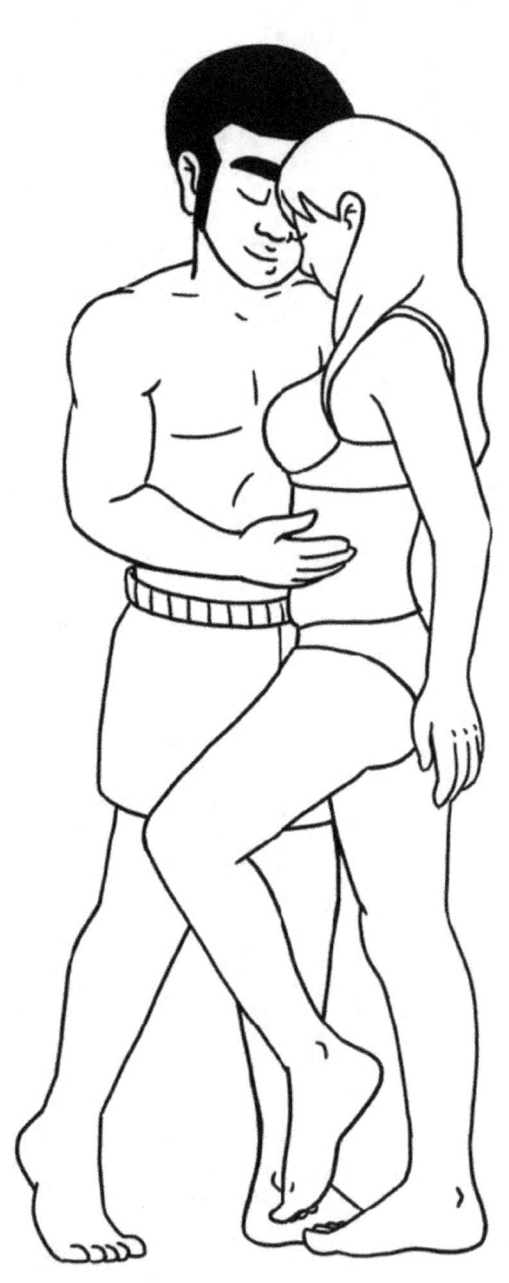

Sex

Make no mistake about it; sex for most partners, the most important things in a committed relationship. More relationships fall apart because of sexual dissatisfaction than any other factor. If a partner is dissatisfied with sex in the relationship, they may seek it out in other partners.

Many people who have been married for years, have children and stayed married because of their faith and values, but did not enjoy sex with their partner have committed adultery and left the relationship.

Here is another example of where Notes could have created a dialog with what each likes in sex, discussing and planning exchanges and others related topics. Keep in mind that you have to approach this communication tool with an open mind and willingness to communicate and trust each other no matter what the other writes, as it's simply about strengthening your partnership.

Name:
Date:
Time:
Mood:
Comments:

Name:
Date:
Time:
Mood:
Comments:

Name:
Date:
Time:
Mood:
Comments:

Name:
Date:
Time:
Mood:
Comments:

Name:
Date:
Time:
Mood:
Comments:

Name:
Date:
Time:
Mood:
Comments:

Name:
Date:
Time:
Mood:
Comments:

Name:
Date:
Time:
Mood:
Comments:

Name:

Date:

Time:

Mood:

Comments:

Name:

Date:

Time:

Mood:

Comments:

Name:

Date:

Time:

Mood:

Comments:

Name:

Date:

Time:

Mood:

Comments:

Name:
Date:
Time:
Mood:
Comments:

Name:
Date:
Time:
Mood:
Comments:

Name:
Date:
Time:
Mood:
Comments:

Name:
Date:
Time:
Mood:
Comments:

Name:
Date:
Time:
Mood:
Comments:

Name:
Date:
Time:
Mood:
Comments:

Name:
Date:
Time:
Mood:
Comments:

Name:
Date:
Time:
Mood:
Comments:

Name:
Date:
Time:
Mood:
Comments:

Name:
Date:
Time:
Mood:
Comments:

Name:
Date:
Time:
Mood:
Comments:

Name:
Date:
Time:
Mood:
Comments:

Name:
Date:
Time:
Mood:
Comments:

Name:
Date:
Time:
Mood:
Comments:

Name:
Date:
Time:
Mood:
Comments:

Name:
Date:
Time:
Mood:
Comments:

Name:
Date:
Time:
Mood:
Comments:

Name:
Date:
Time:
Mood:
Comments:

Name:
Date:
Time:
Mood:
Comments:

Name:
Date:
Time:
Mood:
Comments:

Name:

Date:

Time:

Mood:

Comments:

Name:

Date:

Time:

Mood:

Comments:

Name:

Date:

Time:

Mood:

Comments:

Name:

Date:

Time:

Mood:

Comments:

Name:
Date:
Time:
Mood:
Comments:

Name:
Date:
Time:
Mood:
Comments:

Name:
Date:
Time:
Mood:
Comments:

Name:
Date:
Time:
Mood:
Comments:

Name:
Date:
Time:
Mood:
Comments:

Name:
Date:
Time:
Mood:
Comments:

Name:
Date:
Time:
Mood:
Comments:

Name:
Date:
Time:
Mood:
Comments:

Name:
Date:
Time:
Mood:
Comments:

Name:
Date:
Time:
Mood:
Comments:

Name:
Date:
Time:
Mood:
Comments:

Name:
Date:
Time:
Mood:
Comments:

Name:
Date:
Time:
Mood:
Comments:

Name:
Date:
Time:
Mood:
Comments:

Name:
Date:
Time:
Mood:
Comments:

Name:
Date:
Time:
Mood:
Comments:

Name:
Date:
Time:
Mood:
Comments:

Name:
Date:
Time:
Mood:
Comments:

Name:
Date:
Time:
Mood:
Comments:

Name:
Date:
Time:
Mood:
Comments:

Name:
Date:
Time:
Mood:
Comments:

Name:
Date:
Time:
Mood:
Comments:

Name:
Date:
Time:
Mood:
Comments:

Name:
Date:
Time:
Mood:
Comments:

Name:
Date:
Time:
Mood:
Comments:

Name:
Date:
Time:
Mood:
Comments:

Name:
Date:
Time:
Mood:
Comments:

Name:
Date:
Time:
Mood:
Comments:

Politics

Like religion, this is a topic that can divide people pretty sharply. My advice here is the opposite from the faith chapter: you don't have to talk about it. Obviously, if you're completely opposed on major issues, you may not be as compatible with your partner as you hoped.

But if that's the case and you still want to be with that person, you don't have to discuss politics. Just agree with your partner that it's a topic that's out of bounds and stick to that, no matter how tempting it is. Another example of how Notes can help; heated topics can be exchanged, notices can be left for rallies etc.

Keep in mind that you have to approach this communication tool with an open mind and willingness to communicate and trust each other no matter what the other writes as it's simply about strengthening your partnership.

Name:

Date:

Time:

Mood:

Comments:

Name:

Date:

Time:

Mood:

Comments:

Name:

Date:

Time:

Mood:

Comments:

Name:

Date:

Time:

Mood:

Comments:

Name:
Date:
Time:
Mood:
Comments:

Name:
Date:
Time:
Mood:
Comments:

Name:
Date:
Time:
Mood:
Comments:

Name:
Date:
Time:
Mood:
Comments:

Name:

Date:

Time:

Mood:

Comments:

Name:

Date:

Time:

Mood:

Comments:

Name:

Date:

Time:

Mood:

Comments:

Name:

Date:

Time:

Mood:

Comments:

Politics

Name:
Date:
Time:
Mood:
Comments:

Name:
Date:
Time:
Mood:
Comments:

Name:
Date:
Time:
Mood:
Comments:

Name:
Date:
Time:
Mood:
Comments:

Name:
Date:
Time:
Mood:
Comments:

Name:
Date:
Time:
Mood:
Comments:

Name:
Date:
Time:
Mood:
Comments:

Name:
Date:
Time:
Mood:
Comments:

Name:
Date:
Time:
Mood:
Comments:

Name:
Date:
Time:
Mood:
Comments:

Name:
Date:
Time:
Mood:
Comments:

Name:
Date:
Time:
Mood:
Comments:

Name:
Date:
Time:
Mood:
Comments:

Name:
Date:
Time:
Mood:
Comments:

Name:
Date:
Time:
Mood:
Comments:

Name:
Date:
Time:
Mood:
Comments:

Name:
Date:
Time:
Mood:
Comments:

Name:
Date:
Time:
Mood:
Comments:

Name:
Date:
Time:
Mood:
Comments:

Name:
Date:
Time:
Mood:
Comments:

Name:

Date:

Time:

Mood:

Comments:

Name:

Date:

Time:

Mood:

Comments:

Name:

Date:

Time:

Mood:

Comments:

Name:

Date:

Time:

Mood:

Comments:

Name:
Date:
Time:
Mood:
Comments:

Name:
Date:
Time:
Mood:
Comments:

Name:
Date:
Time:
Mood:
Comments:

Name:
Date:
Time:
Mood:
Comments:

Name:
Date:
Time:
Mood:
Comments:

Name:
Date:
Time:
Mood:
Comments:

Name:
Date:
Time:
Mood:
Comments:

Name:
Date:
Time:
Mood:
Comments:

Name:
Date:
Time:
Mood:
Comments:

Name:
Date:
Time:
Mood:
Comments:

Name:
Date:
Time:
Mood:
Comments:

Name:
Date:
Time:
Mood:
Comments:

Name:
Date:
Time:
Mood:
Comments:

Name:
Date:
Time:
Mood:
Comments:

Name:
Date:
Time:
Mood:
Comments:

Name:
Date:
Time:
Mood:
Comments:

Name:
Date:
Time:
Mood:
Comments:

Name:
Date:
Time:
Mood:
Comments:

Name:
Date:
Time:
Mood:
Comments:

Name:
Date:
Time:
Mood:
Comments:

Name:
Date:
Time:
Mood:
Comments:

Name:
Date:
Time:
Mood:
Comments:

Name:
Date:
Time:
Mood:
Comments:

Name:
Date:
Time:
Mood:
Comments:

Name:
Date:
Time:
Mood:
Comments:

Name:
Date:
Time:
Mood:
Comments:

Name:
Date:
Time:
Mood:
Comments:

Name:
Date:
Time:
Mood:
Comments:

Shared notes in this book and after reading, the next step you want to do is set down together and read all of the notes you both wrote from the start. All the Notes emotions you shared over time and how you intimately expressed those emotions will bring you closer together as you reread them.

It Just Works That Way; To Continue Growing and Loving Together, You Can Purchase Notes-Partner Relationship Log, 100 Page Log Book at www.houstonepublishing

Conclusion

After reading my advice, you'll probably conclude that it comes down to variations of the first two points: honesty and communication. Be your best self with your partner, make sure they know what's going on in your mind, especially if it might cause problems, and remember to respect them wherever there might be a conflict. You don't have to agree with your partner all the time, as long as you're emotionally available to support them and let them know that you love them no matter what they believe in. Explore Notes-Partners Relationship Log, a perfect way to commutate intimately at the end of this book.

And finally, a piece of advice from my father: if two people live together or share their lives in some way and claim they never argue or disagree, they're lying and/or kidding themselves. Conflicts and disagreements happen, it's the way you work through them, and that matters.

www.ingramcontent.com/pod-product-compliance
Lightning Source LLC
Chambersburg PA
CBHW070423010526
44118CB00014B/1878